The
No Egg Collection
of Simple Cakes, Biscuits and Puddings

Maureen Inwood

ATHENA PRESS
LONDON

The No Egg Collection
of Simple Cakes, Biscuits and Puddings
Copyright © Maureen Inwood 2004

All Rights Reserved

ISBN 1 84401 233 6

First Published 2004 by
ATHENA PRESS
Queen's House, 2 Holly Road
Twickenham, TW1 4EG
United Kingdom

Printed for Athena Press

The
No Egg Collection
of Simple Cakes, Biscuits and Puddings

Foreword

It was discovered I was allergic to eggs at quite an early age. With the help of my Grandmother and some of her eggless wartime recipes, I was able to eat certain biscuits, cakes and puddings. As I grew older I learned to cope with the problem by changing other recipes to suit me, and of course in the process I compiled an egg-free collection of biscuits, cakes and puddings.

Over the years, I have made some discoveries about egg-free baking, which may help you to adapt and invent your own recipes:

- When baking, instead of using eggs in biscuits, cakes and puddings, use a mixture of bicarbonate of soda stirred into milk and/or water. Add to the cake mixture and beat thoroughly.

- Alternatively, bicarbonate of soda can be added straight to the flour before mixing.

Contents

Part One
Cakes

Part Two
Biscuits

Part One
Cakes

IRISH ORANGE FRUIT CAKE

225 g (8 oz) self-raising flour
50 g (2 oz) butter or margarine (soft tub)
125 g (4 oz) demerara sugar
175 g (6 oz) sultanas
1 orange, grated, and some juice (about 25 ml/1 fl oz)
½ teaspoon bicarbonate of soda
150 ml (5 fl oz) milk

Grease a round, 20 cm (8-inch) cake tin. Rub the butter into the flour, add all dry ingredients. Add the grated orange peel and juice. Mix well.

Stir the bicarbonate of soda into the milk. Add to the dry ingredients. Mix well. Turn into cake tin.

Bake in a moderate oven, gas mark 4, 180°C (350°F), for 45 minutes or until golden brown.

1916 TRENCH CAKE

225 g (8 oz) self-raising flour
125 g (4 oz) margarine (soft tub)
75 g (3 oz) demerara sugar
75 g (3 oz) sultanas or currants
2 teaspoon cocoa
1 teaspoon mixed spice
½ teaspoon bicarbonate soda
1 teaspoon vinegar
150 ml (¼ pint) milk

Grease a 20 cm (8-inch) cake tin. Rub the margarine into the flour. Add the dry ingredients. Mix well.

Add the bicarbonate of soda to the milk and vinegar. Beat well into dry ingredients. Turn into cake tin.

Bake in a moderate oven at gas mark 4, 180°C (350°F), for about 1 hour, until firm to touch.

GINGER CAKE

450 g (1 lb) plain flour
3 level teaspoons ground ginger
3 level teaspoons baking powder
1 level teaspoon bicarbonate of soda
1 level teaspoon salt
225 g (8 oz) demerara sugar
175 g (6 oz) butter (or soft tub margarine)
175 g (6 oz) black treacle
175 g (6 oz) golden syrup
300 ml (½ pint) milk

Grease a 23 cm (9-inch) square cake tin about 6 cm (2-inch)
deep. Line well with greaseproof paper. Put all dry ingredients
into a bowl except the sugar. Warm the sugar, butter, treacle
and syrup in a pan over a low heat until the butter has melted.
Stir the melted ingredients into the centre of the dry and mix
together with the milk. Beat thoroughly with a wooden spoon.
Pour the mixture into the tin. Bake in the centre of the oven at
gas mark 4, 180°C (350°F), for about 1 hour 10 minutes. Cut
into squares when cool.

SYRUP LOAF

25 g (4 oz) self-raising flour
½ teaspoon bicarbonate of soda
a pinch of salt
2 tablespoons golden syrup
150 ml (¼ pint) milk

Sift the flour, bicarbonate of soda and salt into a bowl. Heat the syrup and milk until just melted. Pour over the flour and beat well. Pour mixture into a well-greased loaf tin and bake in the centre of a moderate to hot oven at gas mark 5, 190°C (375°F), for 30 minutes or until firm. Slice and serve with butter if desired.

FLAPJACKS

125 g (4 oz) butter or margarine (soft tub)
25 g (1 oz) caster sugar
2 tablespoons golden syrup
225 g (8 oz) rolled oats
¼ teaspoon salt

Grease a Swiss roll tin. Melt the butter, sugar and syrup in a pan. Take off the heat. Add the oats and salt. Mix well. Spread in tin and bake in moderate oven, gas mark 4 180°C (350°F), for 30 minutes until golden brown. Cut into squares and leave in the tin until cooled.

Date Loaf

50 g (2 oz) butter or margarine (soft tub)
125 g (4 oz) brown sugar
225 g (8 oz) self-raising flour
1 teaspoon baking powder
½ teaspoon bicarbonate of soda
150 ml (6 fl oz) milk
1 teaspoon vanilla essence
125 g (4 oz) chopped walnuts
225 g (8 oz) dates (stoned) chopped

Grease a loaf tin. Cream the butter until soft, add the sugar and beat until light. Add the flour and baking powder.

Mix the bicarbonate of soda with the milk and add to the flour and fat mixture, beating well. Add the vanilla essence, walnuts and dates. Turn into the tin. Bake on the middle shelf of a moderate oven, gas mark 4, 180°C (350°F), for about 1 hour until firm to touch.

Raisin Cake

450 g (1 lb) self-raising flour
75 g (3 oz) lard or margarine (vegetable lard or soft tub)
175 g (6 oz) brown sugar (demerara)
300 g (12 oz) raisins
125 g (4 oz) currants or mixed peel
½ teaspoon mixed spice
2 tablespoons marmalade
300 ml (½ pint) milk
1 teaspoon bicarbonate of soda (mixed into the milk)

Grease a 20 cm (8-inch) round cake tin. Rub the lard or margarine into the flour. Add all the dry ingredients and marmalade. Add the milk and beat into a thick batter. Put into tin. Bake on the middle shelf at gas mark 4, 180°C (350°F), for 1¼ to 1½ hours until firm to the touch.

Spice & Sultana Cake

50 g (2 oz) lard or margarine (vegetable lard or soft tub)
175 g (6 oz) demerara sugar
125 g (4 oz) mixed peel, or currants
125 g (4 oz) sultanas
1 teaspoon mixed spice
½ teaspoon ground ginger
1½ cup hot water
450 g (1 lb) self-raising flour
2 teaspoons vinegar
1 teaspoon bicarbonate of soda

Grease a deep roasting tin. Place the lard or margarine, sugar, peel, sultanas, mixed spice and ginger in the hot water and boil for 5 minutes. Remove from heat and cool. Add the flour and vinegar. Mix well.

Mix the bicarbonate of soda with a tablespoon of hot water. Mix into cake mixture. Place into tin. Bake on the middle shelf at gas mark 4, 180°C (350°F), for 1½ hours or until firm. Cool, and cut into slabs or fingers.

Part Two
Biscuits

SHORTBREAD

125 g (4 oz) butter
50 g (2 oz) caster sugar
125 g (4 oz) plain flour
50 g (2 oz) ground rice

Grease a large baking tray. Cream the butter until soft. Add the caster sugar and beat until pale and fluffy. Stir in the flour and ground rice until the mixture blends together. Knead well. Put onto a floured surface and roll out the dough thinly. With a biscuit cutter (7½ cm, 3 inches) cut out about 20 rounds, re-rolling the dough when necessary.

Place on the baking sheet and prick round with a fork. Bake in the oven at gas mark 4, 180°C (350°F), for about 15 minutes or until a pale golden colour. When cool, dredge with caster sugar.

Chocolate Biscuits

50 g (2 oz) margarine (soft tub)
125 g (4 oz) self-raising flour
50 g (2 oz) caster sugar
25 g (1 oz) cocoa
1 tablespoon golden syrup
1 teaspoon bicarbonate of soda
1 teaspoon vanilla essence

Melt the margarine and syrup until tepid, then mix into the flour, cocoa, bicarbonate of soda and vanilla essence. Beat well. Roll out and cut into squares or rounds with a cutter. Place on a greased baking sheet and prick tops with a fork. Bake in the oven at gas mark 4, 180°C (350°F), for about 15 minutes. When cold, sandwich together with chocolate spread or chocolate butter icing.

CHOCOLATE OAT BISCUITS

25 g (1 oz) margarine (soft tub)
25 g (1 oz) cooking fat (or vegetable lard)
225 g (8 oz) self-raising flour
a pinch of salt
125 g (4 oz) rolled oats
50 g (2 oz) sugar
40 g (1½ oz) cocoa
a little milk and water

Grease a large baking sheet. Rub the fats into the flour. Add
the oats, sugar, salt and cocoa. Add a little milk and water, just
to moisten and bind the mixture together. Put onto a floured
surface and roll out thinly. Cut into rounds and prick with a
fork. Place on baking tray and bake in the oven at gas mark 4,
180°C (350°F), for about 15 minutes or until golden brown.

GYPSY CREAMS

225 g (8 oz) rolled oats
125 g (4 oz) plain flour
50 g (2 oz) sugar
1 teaspoon bicarbonate of soda
50 g (2 oz) margarine (soft tub)
50 g (2 oz) lard (or vegetable lard)
1 tablespoon syrup
1 tablespoon water

Grease a large baking sheet. Mix all the dry ingredients in a bowl. Melt the fats, syrups and water – do not boil. Add to the dry ingredients and mix together to a stiff consistency. Make into small balls and flatten slightly (about the size of a ten pence piece). Place on baking tray and bake in the oven, gas mark 4, 180°C (350°F), for 10 to 15 minutes, or until golden brown. When cool, sandwich together with vanilla butter icing.

OATMEAL BISCUITS

125 g (4 oz) self-raising flour
125 g (4 oz) oatmeal
½ teaspoon salt
½ teaspoon baking powder
50 g (2 oz) butter or margarine (soft tub)
1 teaspoon sugar
a little milk and water to mix

Grease a large baking sheet. Mix the flour, oatmeal, salt and baking powder. Rub in the margarine or butter, add the sugar. Mix to a stiff dough with the milk and water. Place on a floured surface and roll out to a thickness of 1½ cm (½ inch). Cut into rounds with a biscuit cutter. Place onto baking sheet and bake in the oven, gas mark 4, 180°C (350°F), for about 15 minutes or until firm to the touch.

OATIE MACAROONS

125 g (4 oz) self-raising flour
125 g (4 oz) rolled oats
75 g (3 oz) butter or margarine (soft tub)
50 g (2 oz) sugar
1 tablespoon golden syrup
½–1 teaspoon almond essence
a little milk to mix

Makes about 15

Grease a large baking tray. Cream the butter or margarine, sugar, almond essence and syrup. Add the flour and oats to the creamed mixture. Mix together with just enough milk to bind. Roll into balls and put onto baking tray, allowing room to spread. Bake for 15 to 20 minutes at gas mark 4, 180°C (350°F), or until golden brown

VIENNESE FINGERS

125 g (4 oz) butter or margarine (soft tub)
25 g (1 oz) icing sugar
125 g (4 oz) plain flour
¼ level teaspoon baking powder
a few drops of vanilla essence
50 g (2 oz) plain chocolate

Beat the butter or margarine until smooth. Add the icing sugar, heating until light and fluffy. Sift in the flour and baking powder. Beat well and add the vanilla essence. Put into a piping bag with a medium star nozzle. Pipe finger shapes about 7½ cm (3 inches) long, onto greased baking sheets spacing well apart. Bake at gas mark 5, 190°C (375°F), for 15 to 20 minutes.

Break up chocolate and place in a bowl over a pan of hot water. When melted, dip ends of biscuits in the chocolate. Leave to set on a wire rack. Dust with icing sugar if desired.

DATE CRUNCHIES

175 g (6 oz) self-raising flour
175 g (6 oz) semolina
175 g (6 oz) butter or margarine (soft tub)
75 g (3 oz) caster sugar
225 g (8 oz) dates (stoned), chopped
1 level teaspoon honey
1 tablespoon lemon juice
a pinch of ground cinnamon

Grease a shallow 18 cm (7-inch) square tin. Mix the flour with the semolina. Melt the butter with the sugar in a saucepan over a low heat, then stir into the flour mixture. Press half of this 'shortbread mixture' into the prepared tin.

Heat the dates with the honey, 4 tablespoons of water, the lemon juice and cinnamon, stirring well until the mixture is soft and smooth. Spread the filling over the mixture in the tin. Cover with the remaining 'shortbread mixture' and press down lightly. Bake, gas mark 4, 190°C (375°F), for 30 to 35 minutes. Cut into fingers and leave in the tin until cooled.

WALNUT BISCUITS

225 g (8 oz) soft margarine
50 g (2 oz) icing sugar
200 g (7 oz) plain flour
150 g (5 oz) corn flour
a few drops of vanilla essence
50 g (2 oz) finely chopped walnuts

Grease a large baking sheet. Cream the margarine and icing sugar together in a bowl until light and fluffy. Beat in the flour and vanilla essence, add the chopped walnuts. Beat until the mixture is soft.

Put into a piping bag with a 1 cm (½-inch) star nozzle. Pipe 5 cm (2-inch) stars onto the baking sheet, leaving room for spreading.

Bake in the oven at gas mark 5, 190°C (375°F), for about 20 minutes or until pale golden. When cool, dredge with icing sugar (if desired).

GINGER BISCUITS

125 g (4 oz) golden syrup
50 g (2 oz) butter or block margarine
rind of 1 orange, finely grated
2 tablespoon of orange juice
175 g (6 oz) self-raising flour
1 level teaspoon ground ginger

Grease one large or two small baking sheets. Place the syrup, butter and sugar in a medium-sized saucepan. Add the orange juice and rind. Heat gently until the ingredients have completely melted. Stir together and leave to cool slightly. Add flour and ginger. Mix thoroughly until smooth. Place small spoonfuls of the mixture onto the baking sheet. Leave room for spreading. Bake in the oven at gas mark 4, 180°C (350°F), for about 12 minutes until golden brown. Leave for a minute or two before easing off the baking sheet with a palette knife.

Part Three
Puddings

BLANCMANGE

4 level tablespoons corn flour
600 ml (1 pint) milk
a strip of lemon rind
3 level tablespoons sugar

Blend the corn flour with a little of the milk. Put the remaining milk in a saucepan with the lemon rind and bring to the boil. Remove lemon rind. Pour the corn flour paste onto the milk, stirring all the time. Bring back to the boil and when the mixture thickens, add sugar to taste. Cook for about two minutes. Remove from heat. Pour into a dampened 600 ml (1 pint) jelly mould and leave to cool and refrigerate until set. Turn out to serve.

Variations
Omit the lemon rind, substituting with 50 g (2 oz) grated chocolate or 15 to 30 ml (1–2 tablespoons) coffee essence added to the cooked mixture.

JUNKET

600 ml (1 pint) pasteurised cow's milk
1 level tablespoon caster sugar
2 teaspoons rennet essence
grated nutmeg (optional)

Heat the milk in a saucepan until just warm to the finger.
Remove from the heat and stir in the sugar until dissolved.
Add the rennet, stirring very, very gently. Pour into a shallow
dish and leave undisturbed for 1–1½ hours until set. Can be
chilled in the fridge when set. Add nutmeg to serve (optional).

MINCEMEAT FLAN

75 g (3 oz) lard or vegetable lard
175 g (6 oz) self-raising flour
a pinch of salt
50 g (2 oz) oatmeal or rolled oats
a little water
441 g (14½ oz) mincemeat

Rub the lard into the flour until fine, then add the salt and oatmeal or rolled oats. Add enough water to make a stiff dough. Roll out as ordinary pastry. Line a pie or flan dish and crinkle the edges. Spread the mincemeat over the pastry. With any leftover pastry, cut out shapes with a cutter or knife and place them on top of the flan. Bake in the middle of the oven at gas mark 5, 190°C (375°F), for about 25 minutes until the pastry is golden brown.

SPONGE PUDDING

50 g (2 oz) margarine (soft tub)
175 g (6 oz) self-raising flour
50 g (2 oz) sugar
1 tablespoon golden syrup
½ teaspoon bicarbonate of soda
1 dessertspoon vinegar
milk, to mix

Rub the margarine into the flour and then add the sugar and golden syrup. Blend the bicarbonate of soda with the vinegar. Add to the flour mixture, with enough milk to make a sticky consistency. Put the mixture into a greased pudding basin and cover with greaseproof paper and a tin foil lid.

Steam for about 1½ hours. Serve with fruit, jam and/or custard (without covering can be microwaved for 6½ minutes in medium, 700-watt oven).

Variations
Add 25 g (2 oz) cocoa powder to the mixture.
Put golden syrup or jam in the bottom of the pudding basin and put the mixture on top. Steam as above.

RHUBARB BREAD PUDDING

large tin of rhubarb or 450 g (1 lb) fresh rhubarb
stale bread and butter or low fat spread
golden syrup
1 teaspoon vanilla essence

Cover the bottom of a casserole dish with golden syrup. Put a
layer of quartered bread and butter on the syrup. Add a layer of
sweetened rhubarb. Add the vanilla essence. Place a layer of
bread and butter on top. Bake in a hot oven, gas mark 7, 220°C
(425°F), for about 15 minutes. Served with custard or cream.

Spiced Apple Pie

Filling:
450 g (1 lb) cooking apples
75 g (3 oz) sugar
the rind of 1 lemon
½ teaspoon mixed spice

Pastry:
75 g (3 oz) self-raising flour
75 g (3 oz) corn flour
75 g (3 oz) butter or margarine (soft tub)
50 g (2 oz) caster sugar
a pinch of salt
a little milk

Stew the apples with a little water and the sugar, lemon and spice until turned into a pulp.

To make the pastry sieve all the dry ingredients into a bowl and rub in the butter or margarine until it has the fine appearance of bread crumbs. Add enough milk to mix well and until a stiff mixture is obtained. Knead on a floured board, roll out and line a pie or tart tin with half of the pastry. Add the apple pulp and cover with the rest of the pastry. Bake in the oven for about 40 minutes at gas mark 5, 190°C (375°F), or until golden brown. Dust with caster sugar.

FRUIT CRUMBLE

50 g (2 oz) butter or margarine (soft tub)
125 g (4 oz) plain flour or self-raising flour
125 g (4 oz) sugar
450 g (1 lb) fruit (sliced apples, sliced peaches, rhubarb, plums,
gooseberries, apricots, pears, blackberries)

Rub the butter or margarine into the flour until the mixture resembles fine bread crumbs, then stir in half the sugar. Arrange half the fruit in a pie dish and sprinkle with the remaining sugar. Top with remaining fruit. Spoon the crumble mix over the fruit and lightly press down. Bake in the oven for about 45 minutes at gas mark 4, 180°C (350°F), until pale golden. Serve with custard or cream.

FRESH FRUIT FLAN

50 g (2 oz) margarine (soft tub)
1 dessertspoon golden syrup
125 g (4 oz) self-raising flour
1 level teaspoon baking powder
fresh fruit (gooseberries, blackberries, strawberries, raspberries, black
currants, red currants)
1 packet fruit gelatine

Cream the margarine, sugar and syrup until pale and light. Add the flour and baking powder. If the mixture is too thick, add some milk and water mixed. Beat well. Put the mixture into a flan tin. Bake at gas mark 4, 180°C (350°F), for 20 minutes until golden brown. When cooled, arrange chosen fresh fruit on the sponge base (if using apple or banana, dip in lemon juice first). Make up a fruit gelatine and cover the fruit. Serve with fresh cream.

CHOCOLATE PUDDING

50 g (2 oz) butter or margarine (soft tub)
50 g (2 oz) plain chocolate
125 g (4 oz) self-raising flour
1 teaspoon baking powder
175 g (6 oz) caster sugar
150 ml (5 fl oz) milk
50 g (2 oz) sugar (granulated)
50 g (2 oz) soft dark brown sugar
2 heaped tablespoons cocoa

Melt the butter or margarine and chocolate in a small basin over a saucepan of hot water. Put the flour, baking powder and caster sugar in a bowl. Stir in the mixture of butter or margarine and chocolate, along with the milk. Beat until smooth. Put into an ovenproof dish. Mix the sugars and cocoa powder and sprinkle over the pudding mixture. Pour over 150 ml (5 fl oz) water. Cook for about 45 minutes in the oven, gas mark 4, 180°C (350°F), until the top is crispy.

BANANA CREAM PIE

Biscuit Base
75 g (3 oz) butter or margarine (soft tub)
150 g (6 oz) crushed digestive biscuits

Filling
150 g (6 oz) butter or margarine (soft tub)
150 g (6 oz) caster sugar
397 g can condensed milk
2 bananas
300 ml (½ pint) whipping cream (or low fat cream)
grated chocolate or chocolate chips to decorate

To make the base, melt the butter or margarine in a pan, add the crushed biscuits and stir in. Press the mixture into a pie dish. Chill.

For the filling, place the butter or margarine and sugar in a pan, heat gently until the butter or margarine melts. Add condensed milk and boil gently for 5 minutes to make a golden caramel colour. Pour over the biscuit base and let it cool. Slice the bananas and arrange on the caramel. Whip the cream and spread over the bananas. Serve chilled. Decorate with grated chocolate or chocolate chips.

SHORTCRUST PASTRY

225 g (8 oz) plain flour
a pinch of salt
50 g (2 oz) butter or margarine (soft tub)
50 g (2 oz) lard (or vegetable lard)
water to mix

Place the flour and salt in a bowl and add the fats. Using both hands, rub the fat between the finger tips lightly into the flour until the mixture resembles fine bread crumbs. Add water gradually until a stiff dough results. Transfer to a floured surface and knead until all cracks disappear in the pastry. Roll out to required thickness and size. (Can alternatively be made with wholemeal or self-raising flour.)

Part Four
Icings

BUTTER CREAM ICING

75 g (3 oz) butter or margarine, softened
175 g (6 oz) icing sugar
1–2 tablespoons of milk or warm water

Put the butter into a bowl and cream until soft. Sift and
gradually beat in the icing sugar, then add the water or milk
and beat until smooth and thick.

Variations

Chocolate: dissolve 15 ml (1 level tablespoon) of cocoa powder
in a little hot water. Cool before adding to the butter cream
icing.

CHOCOLATE ICING

100g (4 oz) icing sugar
10 ml (2 level tablespoons) cocoa powder
15 ml (1 level tablespoon) hot water

Dissolve the cocoa powder in the hot water, add to the icing sugar and mix well.

Glossary of Terms

Baking powder

A raising agent usually made of cream of tartar and bicarbonate of soda, which react to produce carbon dioxide. This expands during baking and makes cakes rise.

Beating

A method of getting air into mixtures and making sure all ingredients are well mixed, either by hand whisk or electric mixer.

Bicarbonate of soda

Mixed with water or milk, it acts as a raising agent.

Creaming

Beating together fat and sugar until the mixture resembles whipped cream in texture and colour (pale and fluffy).

Custard

Egg-free custards are made by Birds custard, and can be obtained at all good supermarkets.

Dough

A thick mixture of uncooked flour and liquid combined with other ingredients. The term 'dough' is used to refer to mixtures such as pastry, scones and biscuits.

Dredging or dusting

Sprinkling with icing sugar or castor sugar after cooking.

Grease or greasing

Using a little butter, margarine or oil, baking tins are greased to prevent the mixture from sticking when it cooks. Flour is then dusted over the greased tins.

Knead
To work dough by pressing with the heel of the hand, or with the fingertips lightly.

Lukewarm or tepid
Describes the temperature, usually of a liquid, when it is about average body temperature – 37°C/98.4°F.

Piping
Forcing cream, icing or cake mixture through a nozzle fitted onto the end of a nylon or greaseproof paper piping bag.

Rennet
A substance taken from the lining of a cow's stomach, which will curdle milk. It is used for cheese making and junket. Vegetarian rennet is available from health food shops.

Rubbing in
Method of incorporating fat into flour when a short texture is required. It is used for pastry, scones, cakes and biscuits.

Sifting
Passing flour or sugar through a sieve to remove lumps.

Whipping
Beating air rapidly into a mixture, either with a manual or electric whisk.

1701983R0004

Printed in Great Britain
by Amazon.co.uk, Ltd.,
Marston Gate.